The Filth and the Fury

Adapted from the documentary directed by Julien Temple

St. Martin's Griffin
New York

Copyright Acknowledgments:
Photographs of Nat Jackley and Bill Grundy and the Sex Pistols appear courtesy of Pearson Television International. Photograph of Nat Jackley © 1975 Thames Television International. Photograph of Bill Grundy and the Sex Pistols © 1976 Thames Television.

Book design by Margo Mooney, pink design, inc.

ISBN 0-312-26494-1

First Edition: March 2000

10 9 8 7 6 5 4 3 2 1

The Filth and the Fury

SiD ViCiOuS

**WELL, YOU KNO
GIVE A FUCK WI
PUBLIC THINK.**

, LIKE, I DON'T

T THE GENERAL

HERE NOW
BEGINS one
of the most
FAMOUS, and at
the same time
INFAMOUS, of
the legends
that are
attached to
the crownd of
ENGLAND.

JOHn LyDON

POOR. POOR IRISH. LONDON IRISH. People don't like other poor people, and rather than blame the people that make you all poor, you blame each other. Divided we fall, I think is the mentality…You just grow up thinking poor is not acceptable and because of the class system in England [it] makes you extremely angry—all the time, because you're told that you don't stand a chance and you should just accept your lot and get on with it…This chaos [that] was going on in England was because people were fed up with the old way. The old way was clearly not working so they were demonstrating in all sorts of abstract ways: strikes, union officials having their say, et cetera, et cetera. Football violence is part of that too…when you feel powerless, you will grab any power you can to retain some self-respect.

STeve JONes

I WAS BROUGHT UP IN HAMMERSMITH. I was born in Queen Charlotte's hospital on September 3, 1955. And then I lived with my mum in Hammersmith for a few years and then my mother and my stepfather who was…I knew/thought at the time was my dad (my real dad, he bailed when I was two) and then they got a flat in Shepherd's Bush…We lived in a basement flat and I slept at the edge of their bed in a camp bed.

PaUL COOK

WELL, HE [STEVE JONES] WAS KIND OF HOME-LESS, IF YOU'D LIKE. I had a more stable background, obviously. I mean, I'm at home and stuff and working, and Steve didn't live at home—he'd stay around my place or he'd stay around some other place, he'd be sleeping on my floor, or on our other friends' floor, you know what I mean? He wouldn't really go home because he moved to Battersea and he didn't like that, so he'd be over our way and he'd be in and out of various offenders' institutions, you know. So he had more of a wayward lifestyle, obviously, than among us—he'd probably seen more.

Paul Cook as a boy.

Steve JOnes as a child, with monkey.

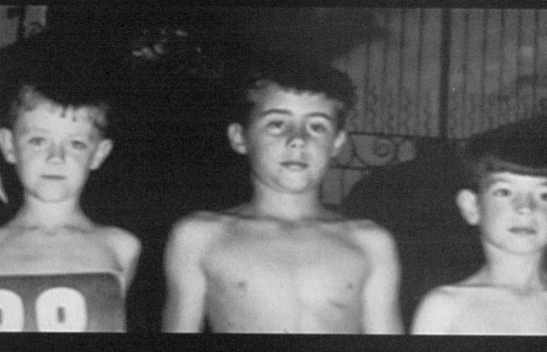

Young Glen Matlock (center).

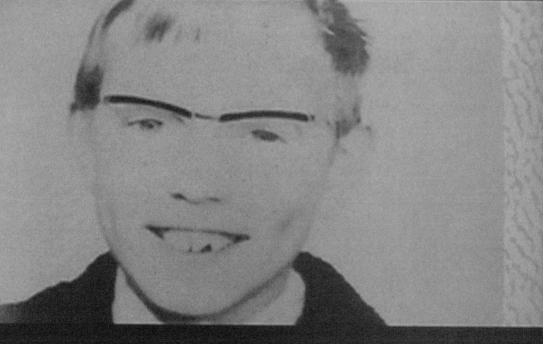

Lad Lydon in specs.

Steve Jones

MY REAL FATHER—I HAVE NO IDEA WHAT HE LOOKS LIKE. I know his name—I found out his name from my mum recently. His name was Don Jarvis, and he was an amateur boxer. And as far as I know he married and had three kids and moved up north somewhere, like Leicestershire or something. I never met him. I'd like to just to see what I looked like—what I come from, you know, or at least a photo or something, you know.

Glen Matlock

YEAH. I was born in London—up to I was about fifteen or sixteen lived in Kents Graham, sort of a suburb. Went to local schools. Me dad was a factory worker; me mum worked in a powder-puff factory. And that was about it, really.

Steve Jones

I ACTUALLY LEFT HOME WHEN I WAS FIFTEEN. I started living with another friend of mine. I used to stay at Paul's [Cook] a lot and I used to stay with this other guy—with his mum and dad. Plus we, we moved to Battersea and what you normally do when you move district is you change schools as well, and I didn't want to make new friends so I traveled from Battersea to Shepherd's Bush to go to school.

John Lydon

IF YOU WERE TO LOOK BACK AT ME AS A SCHOOL KID YOU'D SEE A VERY SHY, QUIET LITTLE CHURCH MOUSE KIND OF A CHARACTER. I was very quiet at school. Up until the age of four-teen or fifteen, when I'd decided I'd had enough. Because what we were being taught I knew we were being fobbed off and basically given a third-rate ver-sion of reality: To not show any hope or prospects. So you would not be capable of questioning your future because you didn't have one. If somebody has to drive the trains, dig the trenches, clean the sewers and—hello?—that was my dictate. [Following a childhood bout of meningitis,] I was completely brain-wiped. There was nothing going on, all mem-ories had been erased. They came back years later, but that's only because my mother stuck with me.

There was no system, no public health, like, nothing to, like help me through that. I was, quite frankly, thrown out of the hospital and left alone and would, no doubt, from there on been treated like an imbecile. Oh, what a tragedy that would have been... there would be no filth and fury!

STeVe JONeS

I REALLY DIDN'T LEARN A LOT AT SCHOOL; OBVIOUSLY, WITH NOT VERY MUCH EDUCATION, I COULDN'T READ AND WRITE VERY GOOD. I attempted a couple of jobs when I left school working for Benham's Heating and Ventilation Company and it was just not my cup of tea just being in boiler rooms getting covered in soot—but I got fired anyway because I got arrested and put in an Approved [reform] school. But, um...I didn't learn fuck-all at school. It was a joke really.

GLeN MaTLOCk

I WAS NEITHER KEEN ON SCHOOL OR INTO IT. I just went for the ride. I didn't really know what I wanted to do, other than working. By then I got interested in the arts and ended up going St. Martin's Art College.

JOHn LyDON

I LOVE READING. It's my favorite thing to do, and Shakespeare I just really got into. I love the absurdity of the characters—there's a cartoon quality to the characters. In a weird way that helped when I joined the Sex Pistols. The whole persona of, say Richard III and the Hunchback of Notre Dame is in there, and just bizarre characters that somehow or other through all their deformities managed to achieve something...It was the absurdity of the image I liked. That image...deformed, hilarious, grotesque, and powerful with a brilliant mind...But he [Richard III] got so that dogs would bark at him whenever he stopped on the street...Well, I've got news for you, dogs bark at me. Now, there's a great connection between me and Richard III—dogs bark at me!

PaUL COOK

I GOT MORE OF AN EDUCATION, I SUPPOSE, AND MORE OF A SOLID FOUNDATION OF WORK, IN ROOTS IN THE WORK ETHIC, I SUPPOSE... I DON'T THINK STEVE GOT THAT. He was never really at school a lot, either...

JOHn LyDON

FOR ALL INTENTS AND PURPOSES I WAS BRAIN-DEAD, AND THAT TOOK TIME AND EFFORT AND A LOT OF HARD WORK, BUT I GOT THERE IN THE END AND THEN I DECIDED I DID NOT ENJOY THE EQUALITY WITH MORONS. I wanted better.

PaUL COOK

STEVE WAS A MUCH WILDER KID THAN I WAS. I was a lot more straight down the line…He was quite wild even then at ten, eleven years old. I think he was always getting into trouble.

JOHn LyDON

STEVE'S IMAGE WAS THIS TOUGH AND HARD GUY, AND IT WAS ALWAYS HILARIOUS TO ME. He always looked like a hairdresser on the high road. He had a perm and, unfortunately, it became permanent.

STeVe JONes

WE USED TO ALWAYS, LIKE, WERE TOTALLY INTO MUSIC, YOU KNOW, ROXY MUSIC AND DAVID BOWIE, AND USED TO GO ROUND TO [PAUL'S] HOUSE AND JUST PLAY RECORDS ALL THE TIME…BUT LATER WE GOT MORE INVOLVED, WE BROKE AWAY FROM THE SKINHEAD LOOK AND WERE INTO, LIKE, THE GLAM LOOK—BOWIE— AND DYED OUR HAIR AND STARTED WEARING THE CLOTHES. We used to go down the Kings Road and watch what was going on and found out where all the rock stars shopped.

John Lydon's mum, who saved his fried brain.

JOHn LyDON

SID'S MUM WAS VERY MIDDLE-CLASS. Ex-junkie, apparently. One of the Ibiza hippy crowd…and his father was—which was the most absurd thing of the lot—was a Grenadier Guard. One of those that looked after Buckingham Palace to save the Queen from the public. And you know, and hello, you know the EMI signing, when we did it that day [in front of Buckingham Palace], Sid's old man could have been one of those guards inside. Heaven. Imagine that Sid's signing a very expensive contract while his old man's on guard inside the fence. It's genius.

JOHn LyDON

STEVE AND PAUL WERE VERY...PAUL WAS FRIENDLY IN A REMOTE KIND OF WAY, HIDING BEHIND STEVE'S AGGRESSIVE ATTITUDE. Steve's aggressive attitude was no threat to me whatsoever. I was interested in them as a group of people because I thought that they were fascinatingly different from each other. And then there's Glen waffling on about nice things like the Beatles.

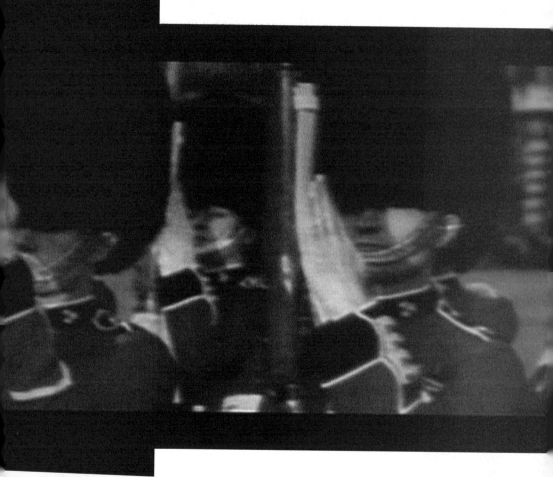

STeVe JONes

I KNOW VERY LITTLE ABOUT GLEN'S FAMILY. I've never seen them. I was never introduced to them. Don't know anything about them. But I think, basically, I think Glen is a very sweet person, he's had a very nice upbringing and he used to get along with everybody.

jOHn LyDOn

WE WERE THE VERY FIRST PEOPLE TO CALL EACH OTHER CUNTS.

PaUL COOk

AND WE WERE VERY INTERESTED IN MUSIC BY THAT TIME, YOU KNOW, AND FASHION AS WELL, WE'D ALWAYS BEEN IN FASHION.

jOHn LyDOn

I SUPPOSE THAT THE WHOLE GREEN HAIR "I HATE PINK FLOYD" THING WAS TO ANNOY AS MANY PEOPLE AS I COULD. Pink Floyd were sacrosanct as the Royal Family then—it was absolutely—no way could you have anything bad to say about such "genius." Well, I thought, "No—wrong." The pomposity of it all. All those superbands at that time. Emerson, Lake and Palmer—yes, they were dinosaurs, they were unrelated to anything but a bunch of spoiled university students.

STeVe JONes

WE THOUGHT THE KINGS ROAD WAS IT, WE USED TO GO DOWN THERE REGULARLY EVERY WEEK REALLY, WE WOULD HIT THE KINGS ROAD AND THEN MALCOLM'S SHOP. We'd always go, that was one of the more exciting elements of Kings Road, we'd end up at his shop every week.

JOHn LyDON

I HAD A LOT OF ANGER, A LOT OF IDEAS. My brain was just waiting for a point and a purpose to hook on to. And the Sex Pistols was a...just happened at exactly the right time for me. I had no idea what I was going to do with my life and by sheer chance of looking absurd on the Kings Road some band wanted to try me out to see if there was more to it than just looks.

STeVe JONes

LIKE I SAID, WE WERE DOWN THE KINGS ROAD EVERY WEEK SO WE WERE ABLE TO SEE MALCOLM [McLaren] **EVERY WEEK, YOU KNOW... IT WAS THE EASIEST ONE OF THE SHOPS WHERE THEY DIDN'T MIND YOU HANGING AROUND AND HAVING A CHAT.** Malcolm had a jukebox there as well, you could listen to music and just generally have a chat with Malcolm.

JOHn LyDON

STEVE AND PAUL STRUCK ME AS JUST REGULAR CHAPS. I know regular chaps. I come from regular chaps. No problem. And I also knew... their lack of respect for Malcolm—because right from minute one they would also be taking the piss out of him. It was a very healthy situation. Because Malcolm is a man—who loves to pontificate a lot—and say how important he is and full of his own self-importance. He's a bit like a politician, really. A liar. Steve and Paul knew that instinctively about him but he manipulated them. In their own dumb way, they still got what they wanted out of him.

PaUL COOK

I DON'T THINK MALCOLM KNEW WHAT WAS GOING ON AT THE TIME, YOU KNOW. It would be up to us to clue him in on what was going on musically at the time, cause he was obviously more into the fashion side of things.

JOHn LyDON

KINGS ROAD AT THE TIME WAS THE FASHION CENTER OF LONDON. People were extremely absurd and still stuck into flares [bell-bottoms] and platform shoes and neatly coiffeured longish hair and just being neat and trendy and superficial and pretending the world wasn't really happening. It was an escapism I resented...I walked up and down the Kings Road with complete anger and resentment to that. "How dare you?" If you don't accept that there's a problem, then you are part of the problem...I expect people to be aware that while you're looking ever so trendy and fashionable and wealthy walking up and down the Kings Road that there was also a garbage strike going on for years and years and years and that there was trash piled ten foot high. They seemed to have missed that. Deal with it. Wear the garbage bag, for God's sake— and then you're dealing with it. And that's what I was doing. I would wrap myself, basically, in trash. Here's the problem. Deal with it.

GLeN MaTLOCk

THE FIRST TIME I MET MALCOLM, HE SPOKE TO ONE GUY IN ONE ACCENT AND TO ANOTHER GUY IN ANOTHER ACCENT. I thought, "Well, this bloke can't make up his mind."

Drinking beer backstage.

JOHn LyDOn

MALCOLM'S SHOP INTERESTED ME BECAUSE OF THE RUBBER WEAR. I just "lurved" the sex-perversion thingy side of it very, very much and found that very appealing. And at the same time, ridiculous—and absolutely untitillating. But fascinating, that people can get themselves into such a predicament that the only way you can have sex is in a face mask and a rubber T-shirt—with a bollock weight. I loved the idea of wearing a rubber shirt. I was poor and I would have to work hard and save up money to get that. Nicking it really wouldn't be any achievement at all. I've never been into thievery.

SiD ViciOus

I DON'T THINK MALCOLM REALLY MANAGED THE GROUP...HE JUST GOT THE GROUP TOGETHER, AND THAT WAS A SMART MOVE, GETTING THAT GROUP TOGETHER. He got the right people together.

PaUL COOK

WELL, WE WERE VERY INTERESTED IN FASHION AND MUSIC. It was very important to us, what was going on in music…Sorry, could you repeat the question?

STeVe JONeS

WE WERE FED UP WITH THE MUSIC SCENE AT THE TIME. It was our nature to start something awkward which was another subculture, if you like. I thought it was too stale in the music scene and all too predictable, really.

He called himself an impresario:
Malcolm McLaren.

PaUL COOK

WHAT GOT US INTERESTED IN FORMING A BAND? I don't know really. We wanted to be in a band, it was five of us hanging around together, and there was Steve, myself, a guy called Jim Macken, Steve Hayes, and the famous Wally Nightingale. And Wally played guitar...

I think it was Wally probably, Wally who said, "Let's join a band, let's start a band," you know, we couldn't play at almost anything, you know, and we just said, at the time, that Steve would be the singer because he was kind of the obvious choice to be singer because he was the most outrageous and whatever. I would be drums, Jim Macken on keyboards, and Steve Hayes would be the bass player. And so it was up to us each of us to go from there and learn our instruments. And the next task was getting the equipment that we wanted, which then comes to Steve.

STeVe JONes

I'D STEAL. I mean, that's all I knew how to do. I used to watch my parents steal at Tesco when I was six. And, you know, I would just follow that. That's what I learnt, you know.

PaUL COOK

HE'S A NICE PROCURER OF GUITARS AND TOYS, AND WHATEVER WE NEEDED, WE MANAGED TO GET THEM AS WELL...MANAGED TO GET GREAT SYSTEMS AND WE COULDN'T PLAY PROPERLY EVEN WHEN WE HAD GREAT GUITARS.

They weren't pOncy rock stars,
but they could still pose:
PaUL COOK, JOHn LyDON, STeVe JONeS on the street.

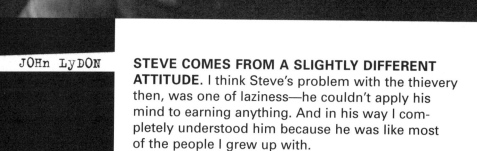

JOHn LyDON

STEVE COMES FROM A SLIGHTLY DIFFERENT ATTITUDE. I think Steve's problem with the thievery then, was one of laziness—he couldn't apply his mind to earning anything. And in his way I completely understood him because he was like most of the people I grew up with.

STeVe JONeS

SHOPLIFTING, STEALING CARS—THAT WAS JUST FOR FUN. I was good at nicking handbags and finding my way into, you know...I didn't just shoplift in Hamley's and Harrods and that; I used to find my way into stockrooms where no one was and I could just take my time...I was good at finding my way around the backs of all these stores and getting into stockrooms and finding an exit where no one saw me. And that's, you know, sneaky...I didn't feel great about breaking into, you know, people's private personal stuff. Even though one of the things I did become good at was going to sports grounds where, you know, these big bastards were playing rugby and football [soccer] and I used to find a way to get into the dressing rooms and steal their wallets. I used to like doing that. I used to go back every week and no one ever cottoned on. No one, you know, said "Gear's missing. Better do something about it next week." I can't believe I didn't get caught and have the shit kicked out of me by these big rugby players.

GLeN MaTLOCk

WE MANAGED TO GET EQUIPMENT FROM ROCK STARS WHO WERE PLAYING AT THE HAMMERSMITH ODEON, WHICH WAS ALWAYS HANDY FOR US, WE'D ALWAYS KNOW OUR WAY ROUND THE BACK. When all the roadies were asleep or whatever, we'd sneak in there and go round and get whatever we needed, really.

PaUL COOK

...AMPLIFIERS, GREAT DRUM KITS, PA SYSTEM— EVERYTHING, YOU KNOW, WHICH WAS A START.

GLeN MaTLOCk

STEVE WAS A BIT OF A KLEPTOMANIAC, REALLY, BECAUSE HE COULDN'T KEEP HIS HANDS IN HIS POCKETS...WHICH IS REALLY QUITE HANDY, CAUSE ONCE WE HAD DECIDED TO FORM A BAND, WE HAD A SORT OF GOAL, YOU KNOW, AND WE FOCUSED ALL OUR ENERGY ON THE BAND AND STEVE WOULD BE TOTALLY OBSESSED ABOUT GOING OUT AND GETTING EQUIPMENT, GUITARS, WHATEVER FOR THE BAND. So before no time at all we had the whole setup.

STeve JONes

WELL, I WAS STEALING ALL THE EQUIPMENT WAY BEFORE WE ATTEMPTED TO PUT THE BAND TOGETHER BECAUSE IT WAS MY...THAT WAS MY CONNECTION TO MUSIC. You know, I couldn't play anything, but that was my way of getting involved in the music.

With Sid at a rehearsal.

JOHn LyDON

THE SEX PISTOLS COULD NEVER HAVE REHEARSED UNLESS THERE WAS NICKED GEAR. I didn't have to contribute to the nicking 'cause most of it was there already. But there were times after, when we'd have to go on little raids and stuff and I'd have to do that in order to continue. It was through necessity, and I understood that. Sheer necessity rather than greed.

PaUL COOk

I'D HAVE MY DRUM KIT SET UP INDOORS, YOU KNOW, IN MY MUM'S BEDROOM, COME HOME EVERY NIGHT FROM WORK, GET UP AND START CRASHING AWAY ON THE DRUMS, ANNOYING THE NEIGHBORS...WE LEARNED TO PLAY AFTER ABOUT SIX MONTHS; WE WERE, LIKE, PUTTING SONGS TOGETHER THEN.

STeVe JONeS WHEN I FIRST PICKED UP THE GUITAR I HAD NO IDEA...THERE WERE JUST TWO RECORDS THAT I PLAYED OVER AND OVER AGAIN AND TRY TO PLAY ALONG TO—ONE WAS THE FIRST NEW YORK DOLLS ALBUM AND ONE WAS IGGY POP—*RAW POWER*—AND I WOULD PLAY IT OVER AND OVER AND OVER AGAIN. Like my finger would like, fucking almost bleed but it didn't matter because I was on the speed and it enabled me to do that. And I guess I did that for like, three months, and the next thing you know, we were playing at St. Martin's College, you know.

JOHn LyDON OH, YOU KNOW WHAT—LISTEN, I MUST TELL YOU ALL OUR FIRST REHEARSALS WERE A NIGHTMARE. It would be constantly, "You know you gotta learn to sing," and it's a "Why? Says who? Why are you accepting all these, like, boundaries?" That's where everything went wrong in the world. Previously.

STeVe JONeS THE FIRST REHEARSALS WERE DEPRESSING AS FUCK. I fucking hated it. I couldn't play guitar. Paul couldn't really keep time...I remember working out a, like, Small Faces song, and the Who's "Substitute." But it was fucking noise...But I stuck in there because I...that's all I had and was no virtuoso on the guitar.

PaUL COOK I MEAN, THERE WAS A LOT OF HUMOR IN THE BAND, ACTUALLY, BECAUSE WE DID LAUGH A LOT IN THOSE REHEARSALS. I don't think we ever took music that seriously, 'cause I thought, we weren't always musicians. Like, I think, you know, we decided as an afterthought to be musicians— and Steve was a very funny guy anyway, you know, he was always cracking jokes.

STeVe JONeS WHEN WE STARTED LEARNING AS A BAND... WE COULDN'T WRITE SONGS, YOU KNOW, SO WE PLAYED ANYTHING...I MEAN, WE EVEN USED TO PLAY SONGS LIKE "BUILD ME UP, BUTTERCUP" BY THE FOUNDATIONS AND "EVERLASTING LOVE" BY THE LOVE AFFAIR AND STUFF LIKE THAT, YOU KNOW, ANYTHING THAT WE'D LIKE, REALLY. It was just a matter of learning our instruments.

GLeN MaTLOCk THOSE FIRST REHEARSALS? They were all right —in for a penny at the time, just to see what we could make of it. You know, we used to play like some covers and things, just to learn to play 'em. Most of which, when we started rehearsing with John, he didn't like. So that had to go.

Malcolm McLaren with Lydon live.

WHAT CAME ABOUT TO ENABLE JOHN TO JOIN THE BAND...MALCOLM WAS GETTING MORE INVOLVED WITH THE BAND, HE WAS COMING DOWN TO WATCH US REHEARSE, ET CETERA, AND IT WAS BECOMING CLEAR THAT STEVE, HOWEVER GOOD, HE WASN'T RIGHT FOR THE FRONT MAN, REALLY. I don't think he wanted to be up there, either, you know. He was getting very good on guitar very quickly, as well, and there was a bit of an ego clash with Wally [Nightingale] already on the guitar part with Steve playing, and Wally, Wally was like, "Don't touch my guitar." After a little bit of conniving we realized that we needed a singer, and I think it was Malcolm's suggestion that Steve should play the guitar: He didn't say, "Get rid of Wally," or anything, but he said, "Steve should play the guitar"...That transpired that sort of clash of egos between two guitars, and it got worse and worse, and eventually we realized that Wally was going to have to go because he was getting a little unbearable, really, and it has lots to do with Malcolm's conniving, as well.

STeVe JONeS SO WE GOT RID OF WALLY AND WE NEEDED A SINGER AND WE THOUGHT WHERE WAS THE BEST PLACE TO FIND ONE—IN MALCOLM'S SHOP. Malcolm says, "I think I found this guy who might be all right for a singer. He's got green hair." I said, "Oh yeah, I know that guy, I've seen him around at the shop, let's try him." We got him down one evening. Malcolm just said, "Would you like to be in a band?" John said, "I can't sing. Just let me sing out of tune, is that all right with you?"

JOHn LyDON WELL, HELLO, MY SEX PISTOL AUDITION BEGAN WITH THEM TRYING TO GET ME DRUNK. Bad mistake. I'm from Irish roots. I don't get drunk. And that not working, then it was, "Ooooh, let's go to the shop and see if you can sing—"fine—knowing I couldn't hold a damn note. And I just did it. I dived in. I test the waters first but then I dove in and then I did extremely well, I thought. See…they didn't know that I knew every Alice Cooper song upside down and backwards and inside out and word for word. "Eighteen" was a song I knew very well.

PaUL COOK WE SWITCHED ON THE JUKEBOX, ALICE COOPER, "EIGHTEEN," AND JOHN WAS PUTTING ON HIS PERFORMANCE, AND JUST…ONCE HE STARTED PERFORMING HE JUST TOTALLY TRANSFORMED HIMSELF INTO JOHN ROTTEN AS WE KNOW HIM—THE CHANGE WAS AMAZING, YOU KNOW, HE JUST WENT INTO HIS TOTAL ACT…I KNEW THERE AND THEN THAT WE FOUND A SINGER STRAIGHTAWAY, NO TWO WAYS ABOUT IT. I think Steve was less sure of him. He was a bit amused by him, looked at him a bit suspiciously, but I was convinced that John would be right one. I don't think Malcolm…I don't know, I think we thought, "Yeah, let's give it a go,"—cause we needed a singer, we had nothing else to lose, so let's go for it.

GLeN MaTLOCk

**MALCOLM COME UP WITH A FEW SUGGES-
TIONS FOR NAMES—ONE OF THEM BEING THE
DAN, ANOTHER, CRÈME DE LA CRÈME, ANOTHER
WAS KID GLAD, AND THE OTHER WAS THE
SEX PISTOLS.** When John got involved, he said,
"What are you going to call yourselves?" and I said,
"The Sex Pistols." And he said, "That is absolutely
outrageous. I am very interested."

STeVe jONes

**JOHN HAD THE ATTITUDE, WHICH WAS OUR
ATTITUDE AS WELL, I THINK—WE ALL HAVE
GENERALLY THE SAME OUTLOOK OF MUSIC,
YOU KNOW, YOU HAD THE ATTITUDE, HE DIDN'T
TAKE IT TOO SERIOUS.** In another way he was
quite serious about music, as well, you know, he
knew his music. He was a music fan like we were,
you know, and he had the raw attitude and the image
as well. John influenced a lot, obviously. I think his
hair was quite short, it was cropped, if I remember
right, but he had his own look together. His clothes
were ill-fitting, they were torn here and there, and
he's dysfunctional, if you like, it's a totally dysfunctional look, which was totally new.

GLeN MaTLOCk

...WE THOUGHT HE WAS KIND OF FUNNY. He
apparently couldn't sing at all at that time. But he
definitely had something going for him. So we
started rehearsing. And then we started rehearsing
a little bit more seriously...

JOHn LyDON

**BASICALLY, I ALWAYS THOUGHT, AFTER EVERY
REHEARSAL, "THESE FUCKS AREN'T GETTING IT."**
Whatever they ultimately, seriously really wanted
in a band wasn't what I wanted. Rehearsals were
difficult, and their friend Malcolm would always,
like, pick them up and they'd go off someplace and
I'd have to go home on the subway. I always felt
alienated inside the Pistols as a band...They never
really allowed me to be a mate.

GLeN MaTLOCk

IT SOUNDS A FUNNY KIND OF THING, BUT I DON'T KNOW WHAT JOHN HAD PLANS TO DO WITH HIS LIFE. I mean, I've places in mind to do painting…Paul was in an apprentice at Wapner's as an electrician and Steve was a thief, but John…

JOHn LyDON

THE TRUTH. I LOVED STEVE'S GUITAR RACKET, BUT RACKET IS WHAT I WANTED. And I know he'd never really get to grips with me as a human being—never did, never will. Paul would always pick up the lyric sheet and go, "Oooh, that's not nice," and run off giggling and that would be the end of that. Glen would always outright go, "Ooooh, you can't sing a song like that—that's not good, you'll offend people."

Sex Pistols

Steve Jones

WE'D START PLAYING LIVE SHOWS BEFORE WE COULD PLAY, REALLY. I mean, we could make noise and some sort of construction of the songs and stuff, but it was madness, it was total madness.

John Lydon

OKAY, HERE WE GO. Early Sex Pistol gigs, right. All the people, like, you know, all the front-row lot, they all ended up in bands, and hence you got the Punk movement. But they got it wrong—they thought it was all about wanting to be a pop star. And that's not what we are interested in at all. And it became horrible—and the name Punk, I've got, like, bitter…a bitter taste in my mouth about it.

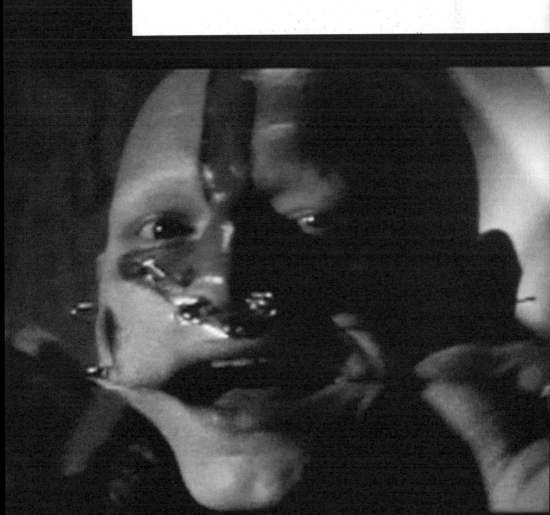

PaUL COOK

THE FIRST GIG THE SEX PISTOLS EVER DID WAS AT ST. MARTIN'S ART COLLEGE WHERE GLEN USED TO BE A STUDENT, AND I THINK HE ARRANGED THE GIG, ACTUALLY. We plug in and start thrashing away, you know, it was total chaos, and they hate us straightaway, the people, they really did hate us and they pulled the plug out on us after about fifteen or twenty minutes and it was nearly a fight, it probably was a fight. And then, in the end, we'd just end up packing up all our equipment and pissing off back down the Charing Cross Road.

JOHn LyDOn

WE DIDN'T REALLY GEL AS A BAND UNTIL OUR FIRST GIG. It was the art college in St. Martin's Lane. The support band was kind of well-known— Bazooka Joe, I think was their name, and they were doing everything they could do to sabotage, threaten, and be antagonistic in every shape and form, and that worked with me no end. But Steve and Paul

didn't like that. Like, you know, they wanted to be everybody's friend and I wanted, like, "Stop it now, let's be everyone's enemy." I left that gig very disappointed with them in terms of their fearfulness.

PaUL COOK

I'M NOT SURE IF SID WAS THERE AT FIRST...I DON'T THINK SO. It was quite frightening at the start, you know, we'd have to stick up for ourselves at all our early gigs, it was quite a tense atmosphere, we needed our mates really, just in case anything happened—because it was tense, people were quite aggressive towards us sometimes, it was quite frightening, and we needed their support.

Steve Jones

I REMEMBER THAT [FIRST GIG] PRETTY WELL.
I remember being just fucking terrified and taking a
Mandrex to calm down. I think I took two Mandrex.
We went up there and it was just a...it was an art
college and it was all these arty fuckers in one
room, there was no stage. And there was this other
band called Bazooka Joe—Adam Ant was the bass
player in it. And we were wandering around knock-
ing the pints back, they were playing the music and
the DJ thing—and then it was time to go on, and
the Mandrex were kicking in and we started playing,
and I just remember looking at John and thinking,
"This is fucking fantastic," and loved it, and it was
like one of those magical moments when everything
in the universe fucking clicked and it was finally,
"This is it, I've made it, we're actually playing in a
band"...Mind you, I was fucked up.

Glen Matlock

**THERE WAS THIS BAND, BAZOOKA JOE, AND I
THINK THEY WERE JEALOUS OF US.** You know,
we seemed more in the know...They pulled the
plugs on us the first show, so obviously we were
getting some sort of reaction.

Steve Jones

MALCOLM WAS THERE, YEAH. He didn't know
what was going on, either, you know, I think he
enjoyed all the chaos.

JOHn LyDON

ALL OF OUR EARLY GIGS WERE PRETTY CHAOTIC LIKE THE FIRST ONE. We'd turn up, just set up, played to a handful of people, pretty much indifferent, sometimes aggressive toward us. It slowly turned around that people, I noticed after the first few gigs, there were a group of people that were interested in what we were doing. They would be standing, come down front and actually listen to what we were doing and very interested in what we were up to. After a handful of gigs, really. It was always something happening, all the early gigs, something would go off. There would always be something going wrong.

STeVe JONeS

ROTTEN,...[LYDON] HE WAS ALWAYS SPITTING ONSTAGE, COUGHING UP GEAR, AND I THINK IT PROBABLY JUST STARTED FROM THAT. He might have gobbed and it went out into the crowd once, accidentally, and the fans see that and think, "Oh, that's good"—and gobbed back. You know, I mean it wasn't something that was invented intentionally... Oh, it was a drag. It was a fucking drag. Getting gobbed in the face, getting saliva hanging off your fucking eyelid. It wasn't pleasant.

JOHn LyDON

ALL ACCIDENTAL. It was all accidental. Most of the things were accidental. The spitting, for instance, that was accidental too. That's because, as you well know, I had meningitis and that affected my sinuses and that would be the way it is for me forever and a day. I have to spit. When I yell my lungs out, gobbing is a perfectly natural attitude. It's not a fashion statement.

JOHn LyDOn

THE GOBBING THING CAME FROM THE *DAILY MIRROR*—I CAN'T BE SURE, PLEASE DON'T SURE ME. But saying that was part of the Punk gig and it was not. If I'm going to be yelling my head at, like, the speed I do, and drink and smoke the amounts I do, this is going to be a natural reaction but I will absolutely tell you outright—you spit at me and I'll absolutely smash your fucking head in. I won't tolerate it, it's not a sign of respect, it's a sign of disrespect. You've got a classic little bit in the docu there of [fashion designer and Malcolm McLaren partner] Vivienne Westwood being spat on. This is not respect. This is knowing fake, bitch. Fake, fake, fake, charging astronomical prices. Fake, phony, fuck off. There's no gobs on me.

JOHn LyDON

THREE-QUARTERS OF OUR LOOK, THAT THIRD-RATE TRAMP THING, THAT WASN'T REALLY STEVE AND PAUL, THAT WAS POVERTY, REALLY. Lack of money. When the arse of your pants falls out you just use safety pins to stick it back on. The fact that that became a fashion statement wasn't deliberate.

STeve JONes

THAT WAS MY INVENTION TO THE SEX PISTOLS, WAS INVENTING THE HANKIE ON THE HEAD.

SiD ViciOus

I DON'T HAVE AN IMAGE. I HAVEN'T GOT AN IMAGE.

JOHn LyDON

I LIKE SID ALL RIGHT. I used to really enjoy the way Sid used to put this vile purple nail polish on his nails. He'd always be too lazy to do it proper, so it would always go up the fingers to the second knuckle, and that's Sid.

John Lydon and Steve Jones live.

SiD ViciOus

...**WE DONE THAT** *TOP OF THE POPS* **THING, AND HE [ROTTEN] WAS GREAT ON THAT, HE WAS FUCKING GREAT, MAN.** There was no need for him to deteriorate. He could hold it...He could have held it together but, no, he just let himself slip. And there was another time that I saw him, and he just dyed his hair black, and I walked in this room and there he was and I said, "Fucking hell, John, you look fantastic"...We were in [lawyer] Steven Fisher's office, I run right over and jumped in his lap and gave him a kiss because he looked so fucking good. And, like, the next day he put all orange dye in it and it looked vile, you know, he fucked it all up, you know, and he was wearing baggy Levi's turned up to there and fucking Paki shoes or something, and you know, he just let himself slip and just became a total embarrassment.

JOHn LyDON   **WE USED TO BUSK FOR MONEY.** Me at a violin, Sid with a tambourine, sometimes a broken guitar, doing Alice Cooper songs. "I Love the Dead" was our favorite—that would get us the most money. "Just please shut up. Here take the money, go somewhere else."

STeVe JONeS   **IT WASN'T NO BIG CONTRIVED EFFORT TO SIT DOWN AND WRITE SOME OF "ANARCHY" OR "GOD SAVE THE QUEEN" OR STUFF LIKE THAT, IT JUST HAPPENED.** It wasn't contrived at all. John would just pick up on things, I think. And, um, the next thing I think John picked up on was the word "anarchy" and we just wrote a song about it, "Anarchy in the U.K."

JOHn LyDON   **THE LYRICS WOULD ALWAYS COME FROM SOMETHING STEVE WOULD PLAY OR WAS LEARNING TO PLAY.** I always focused on his guitaring—as bad or good as it was, it would always get me going somewhere. There was always, like, an out-of-tuneness. An octave up there that shouldn't be there I could focus on, because it's hopeless to ask me to just go, *twang-twang-twang*—sing.

PaUL COOK

JOHN WROTE MOST, THE MAJORITY, OF THE NEXT FOUR SONGS, AND LATER STEVE WROTE THE MAJORITY OF THE MUSIC, AND THAT'S HOW IT WAS. I mean, there's always people who claim that they had an input, but it wasn't—it was totally the band's, the band's doing the music. Malcolm didn't create anything to John. If anything, it was the other way around, I think. Malcolm took a lot of ideas from John and the rest of the band, if you like, bore into him, you know, 'cause John had the look already before he turned up. And, like, Malcolm was always picking our brains about what was going on.

JOHn LyDON

STEVE AND PAUL SLAGGED ME OFF BEHIND MY BACK AT THE START. But then it would shift emphasis, sometimes it would be me and Paul slagging off Steve. There was a time when Steve was a victim. And then it would be me and Steve and Paul and, you know, everybody was united against Glen. That's just the way it was. So that was, in a way, I don't know, a monkeys' tea party.

JOHn LyDON

I ALWAYS WROTE THE LYRICS. I never shared in the band. And that was because I thought that... because they could make some attempt at play I had to double up on my act and not merely sing but get the rest of that stuff together, too. I owed that time on the writing.

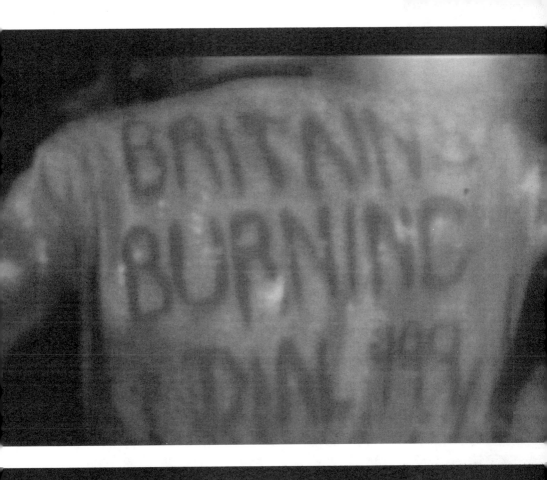

The Bay City Rollers were chart-toppers then.

JOHn LyDON

"ANARCHY IN THE U.K." FOR ME SUMMED UP EXACTLY WHAT WAS GOING ON. There was writing all over the place, there were garbage strikes, and there were strikes on every kind of amenity you could think of. The TV channels would go on and off randomly, total social chaos, and I penned that into "Anarchy in the U.K." I thought "No big deal," myself—the band didn't like the lyrics, they thought "It's not really Bay City Rollers enough" for them. And, in particular, Glen—in fact, that was one of his comments—"We should be more like the Bay City Rollers."

GLeN MaTLOCk

THAT'S ABSOLUTE BOLLOCKS. The only thing I didn't like about "Anarchy" was the dreadful rhyme in it. "Antichrist" used to always make me weep.

JOHn LyDON

I HAVE ONLY ONE THING TO SAY TO ANYBODY THAT SAYS THEY WROTE "ANARCHY IN THE U.K." Liar? The first line I wrote was "I am the antichrist." And I couldn't think of a damn thing that rhymed with it. And then "anarchist" just fitted really nicely. And that be the truth of that. And it was perfect. It was instinctive.

GLeN MaTLOCk

JOHN ALWAYS THOUGHT LIKE A GUY BEING SOME KIND OF FUCKED-UP CATHOLIC.

JOHn LyDON

HE'S [GLEN] A DIFFERENT PERSON NOW. He's gone through a lot and I really respect him. I always did, but I have to be honest at the same time. When you talk like an arsehole and look like an arsehole, you're an arsehole, and, ouch, he fits that so well. Steve and Paul, as far as I know, didn't really want to continue with Glen. They never liked him. The trouble was that Glen wanted it all his way, and it was a very, very dull way. Glen ultimately wanted the Sex Pistols to be more like the Bay City Rollers. And that's a quote from him to me directly. Can you imagine Johnny Rotten singing "Shang-a-lang"?

Glen Matlock.

"God Save the Queen," the SEX PISTOLS' biggest hit, was released to coincide with the silver JUBILEE of Queen Elizabeth II.

STEVE JONES "GOD SAVE THE QUEEN"? I loved it, I thought it was a fucking great rock song. It was great. Had all the elements to it. And I don't really think that what he was singing about was all that outrageous. You know, the lyrics ain't that...You know, he's not saying "Let's kill her" or "Let's fuck her." He was pretty much pointing out what the truth was. You know.

JOHn LyDON YOU DON'T WRITE A SONG LIKE "GOD SAVE THE QUEEN" BECAUSE YOU HATE THE BRITISH PEOPLE. You write it because you love them.

STEVE JONES YOU KNOW, IF THE [Bill] GRUNDY [*Today Show* appearance] THING HADN'T HAPPENED AND WE WROTE THAT SONG AND IT WAS ON A RECORD, I don't thing it would have been such a big stir as it was when all the press came along with it. You know, the *Sun*, the *Daily Mirror*—

TOP 10 SINGL

1	◇	
2		HOTEL CALIFORNIA
3		LOVER BOY
4	●	PEACHES
5		TELEPHONE LINE
6	£	FANFARE FOR THE COMMON MAN
7		O LORI

"You're calling the Queen a moron." It wouldn't
have been such a big thing—git was another thing
to latch on to to sell newspapers.

JOHn LyDON

**"GOD SAVE THE QUEEN" WAS NEVER NUMBER
ONE.** It was number two and there was no number
one that week. They abolished number one...
Welcome to England.

STeVe JONeS

I DIDN'T HAVE A LIFE. I had nothing to lose. And I
was a miserable sod deep down inside. An unhappy
person. So the more havoc created, the more I felt
better at doing it because I was a tortured soul. I
think the fighting came through lack of musical ability.
It was like, "Oh, this is what gets you headlines."

The band when Glen Matlock was still a Pistol.

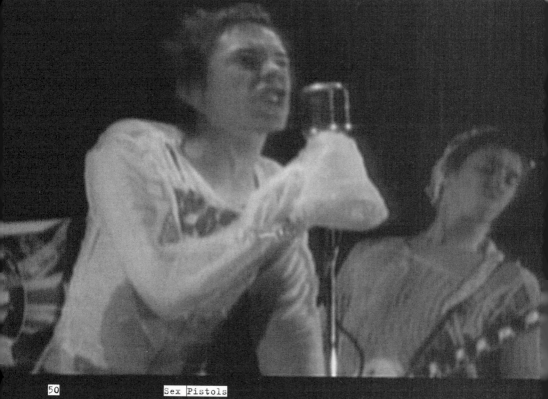

JOHn LyDON

GLEN HATED "GOD SAVE THE QUEEN" WITH A PASSION. Eventually Glen reached a point where he decided outright that the band's direction was absolutely alien to anything he wanted to be associated with, and issued an ultimatum: "Get rid of John or...Good-bye, Glen."

"God Save the Queen" is an abstract song from start to finish. It's not format in any shape or form, yet it sounds right. It's completely pop music and it breaks every rule in the book. There were no hard and fast rules as to songwriting, other than we knew we had to tolerate each other for at least four hours a day.

STeve JONes

I WAS JUST HAPPY WITH THE RIDE. The ride was great, I wasn't really interested in writing new songs. I was just fucking reaping the rewards of what we done. Oh yeah, and Rotten loved it. He loved it. We all loved it. You know—why wouldn't you? I didn't think about the money. I was getting my twenty pounds per week and thinking everything was great. You know, classic rock-and-roll scenario of getting—"Just give them what they want and they'll keep quiet"—and that what was kind of going on. I think Rotten was more on the ball as far as, "Well, where is the money going?" And you know, McLaren at that point was controlling the situation as far as all that...financial things.

Nancy sPunGen

TOTAL DISORGANIZATION. Total Chaos. If you are going to manage a group, you can't have chaos in your management. I mean, Sid still doesn't know how much money he has. He can't get hold of it. He doesn't know how much money he's got. What are you supposed to do?

JOHn LyDON   **WE NEVER ACTUALLY NEVER SAT DOWN TO WRITE PLEASANT LOVE SONGS.** But there would always be that element from Glen. And Malcolm and Glen had a relationship with each other which was always odd to me. Malcolm would always support Glen's nonsense...I have no idea why. None at all. Other than I think that because both of them come from a confused, "Why can't we all be nice?" background. Can I have a beer?

PaUL COOK   **GLEN HAD THIS KIND OF "MOMMY'S BOY" KIND OF IMAGE, YOU KNOW.** I think Glen was being a bit isolated by it all.

GLeN MaTLOCk   **MY MUM ABSOLUTELY HATED THE SEX PISTOLS AND SHE WAS GETTING GRIEF FROM HER FRIENDS AND SHE TOOK IT OUT ON ME.**

JOHn LyDON   **AS PEOPLE, NONE OF US IN THE BAND—APART FROM GLEN, HAD MUCH RESPECT FOR THE POWERS THAT BE...AND ALL THE RULES AND REGULATIONS THAT YOU'RE SUPPOSED TO MERRILY CONTRIBUTE TO.** I was never, for instance, invited to anything, even when the Pistols were like, doing quite well. I would not be invited to parties. I found out years later that was because Malcolm would say, "Don't talk to John. He's a mystery."

PaUL COOK   **REMEMBER, I WAS QUITE CLOSE WITH JOHN.** I always got along quite well with him...and he felt isolated. John wasn't the easiest person to get along with, anyway. I think he would be the first to admit that.

JOHn LyDON

WORDS ARE MY WEAPONS. Violence is something I'm not very good at, because I get tired of the idea of punching someone. It's...it...it doesn't achieve anything at all. If I had any kind of heroes, they'd be people like Gandhi.

GLeN MaTLOCk

YOU KNOW, JOHN'S NOT GOD'S GIFT TO THE WORLD. I think they shot themselves in the foot there. 'Cause I could have gone on and been like really big, instead of just a cult band. I might have a good few albums that sounded good.

JOHn LyDON

THE BAND WAS HELL. IT'S HARD. It's horrible. It's enjoyable to a small degree. But if you know what you're doing it for, you'll tolerate all that because the work at the end of the day is all that matters. We managed to offend all the people we were fucking fed up with. And we went into full attack format. This band wasn't about making people happy, it was about attack. Attack, attack, attack.

SiD ViciOus

I LIKE TO CAUSE A FUCKING RIOT WHEN I DO A GIG. You know what I mean? I don't wanna fucking...you know, I like to incite people to be violent and nasty—so I can be violent back. I like violence. It turns me on.

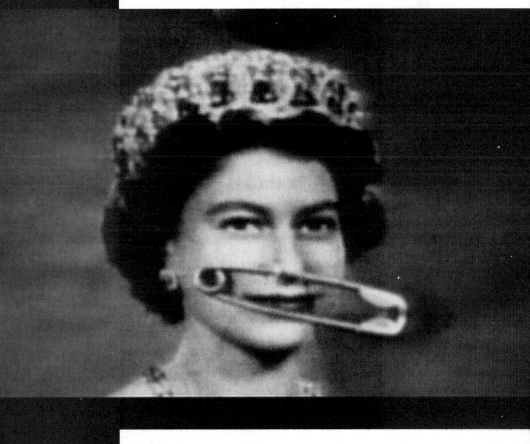

JOHn LvDOn

ONSTAGE...ONSTAGE WE WOULD ALWAYS CLICK. Always click onstage. Always. Paul would follow me and I'd be following Steve. That's how I see it. I think that's the way the Pistols work. There's always a bass player just doing what bass players do, because it's rock music, it isn't reggae. There's no room for great bass-playing on rock music. There just isn't.

Jones, Cook, Lydon.

The
SEX PISTOLS
signed with
EMI on
August 10,
1976.

PaUL COOK

EVERYTHING STARTED HAPPENING REALLY QUICKLY. I MEAN, LOOKING AT IT NOW, IT'S NOT SURPRISING, REALLY, BECAUSE THERE REALLY WASN'T NOTHING DOWN AND ABOUT, AND I THINK THE MUSIC BUSINESS WAS DESPERATE, REALLY, FOR ANOTHER BAND TO COME ALONG AND, LIKE, GIVE EVERYONE A KICK UP THE ASS, WHATEVER. And we had record companies coming down straightaway to see what this new phenomenon was, you know, what they heard about, what was happening on the streets, so we had record companies crawling all over us, really, and eventually we signed with EMI, which was then quite a big deal at the time, you know.

I NEVER THOUGHT, LIKE, LYRICS LIKE "GOD SAVE THE QUEEN" WOULD HAVE THE EFFECT THEY DID: BEING CHASED DOWN THE STREET BY KNIFE-WIELDING HOOLIGANS. Do you think I'd write a song to be a victim of that? I don't fucking think so. Do you think I wrote "Anarchy in the U.K." because I thought that would completely ruin my life? No. Do you think I wrote "Pretty Vacant" so that people would think I was a complete fucking moron? No. It was the fun of the chaos after—fun being fucking dubious. Hard fun.

I MEAN, WE DREAMED IT. WE DREAMT IT. We wanted to be in a band and be successful and all this stuff, but I think we realized it was going to actually be six months, or even a shorter period of time, which is what it was, really. We signed to EMI...yeah, we didn't go, "Oh great we made it, we got money, we're going to be brilliant," all that stuff. We just shrugged our shoulders and got on with it really.

Then Malcolm came in and said, "Quick, we've got a TV show lined up for you because Queen had pulled out, who was also on the EMI label. "Quick, the big car's coming down! Jump in, we're going down to do the *Today Show*—which was a big show at the time. It's just after *The News at Six* or whatever, and they wanted us to do a quick section where we could plug the tour.

The
SEX PISTOLS
appeared on
the *Today
Show*, hosted
by Bill
Grundy, on
December 1,
1976.

PaUL COOK

THE GRUNDY SHOW THEN WAS DONE ON THE SPUR OF THE MOMENT, AND THEY PUT US IN THE GREEN ROOM, WITH EVERYBODY LOOKING AT US STRANGELY. We were having a drink obviously, Steve getting more pissed than anyone, rather quickly, as he did. John was all right, you know. We went on the show and I remember being quite nervous, actually. It was our first TV show, you know, and then we're left with some stroppy guy, Bill Grundy, asking us all these questions: "Uh, well, you've got this money, blah, blah, blah, blah," and "What are you going to do with this?" Basically, he was saying we weren't very good. He, like, never heard of us, obviously—I doubt that he even wanted to do the interview from what he asked us. I think he wanted to get the interview over with as quickly as possible.

STeVe JONeS

HE SLUNG US IN THE GREEN ROOM WITH A FRIDGE, AND I REMEMBER DOWNING ABOUT FUCKING FOUR BOTTLES OF BLUE NUN. We were in there forever. You know, it seems like we were in there for, like, over an hour—two hours, it seemed like—and I was just fucking having a good old time, pissed at this point by the time we went out there...And I remember walking out there through all these wires and all that, and sitting down and they had the fans there—Siouxsie (Sioux of Siouxsie and the Banshees] was one of them—and we were told that he [Bill Grundy] was going to talk to us about the tour and the record and all that. And that's all I remember. The next thing I know he's, like...I got this—picked up his vibe—that he was trying to make us look stupid. And actually, there's a "fuck" word even before they cottoned on to it, because he was drunk himself and he wasn't like, paying attention when he asked, like, "Well, what do you do with the money?" And I said, "We fucking spent it." No one even heard that one until he focused on it later...A bit later on, Rotten... slipped up and said "Shit" under his breath.

Lydon and Jones on the Today Show

JOHn LyDON

STEVE ON THE GRUNDY SHOW ABSOLUTELY TOOK OVER, BECAUSE HE WAS IN HIS ELEMENT. He completely understood that he was just talking, like, to a drunk, as you would a drunk in a pub, and he just topped him. and there was no reason or point for me to butt in or dominate or do anything.

BiLL GRuNDy

I'm told that the group have received forty thousand pounds from a record company. Doesn't that seem...er...to their anti-materialistic way of life?
What will you do with all that money?

STeVe JONeS

We fucking spent it, ain't we? (Grundy does not appear to have heard the response.)

BiLL GRuNDy

Beethoven, Mozart, Bach, and Brahms have all died...

JOHn LyDON

They're all heroes of ours.

BiLL GRuNDy

Really? What?
What were you
saying, sir?

JOHn LyDON

They're wonderful
people.

BiLL GRuNDy

Are they?

JOHn LyDON

Oh yes!
They really turn
us on.

BiLL GRuNDy

Suppose they turn other people on?

JOHn LyDON

(under breath)
Well, that's just their tough shit.

BiLL GRuNDy

It's what?

JOHn LyDON

Nothing.
A rude word.
Next question!

BiLL GRuNDy
_____

> ***No, no!***
> ***What was that***
> ***rude word?***

JOHn LyDON
_____

> ***(childish voice).***
> ***Shit.***

BiLL GRuNDy

> ***Was it really?***
> ***Good heavens,***
> ***you frighten me***
> ***to death.***

JOHn LyDON

*Oh, all right,
Siegfried.*

BiLL GRuNDy

*(to Siouxsie)
Who are you, then?*

SiOuXSie

STeVe JONeS

You dirty old sod.
You dirty old man.

BiLL GRuNDy

Well, keep going,
chief, keep going.
Go on, you've got
another ten seconds.
Say something
outrageous.

STeVe JONeS

You dirty bastard.

BiLL GRuNDy

Go on again.

STeVe JONeS

You dirty fucker!

BiLL GRuNDy

*What a
clever boy.*

STeVe JONeS

You fucking rotter!

2-week
Grundy ov
'filthy' show

WERE THE
PISTOLS
LOADED?

Punk Rock group 'plied
with booze'

d
ets the
brush-off
at home

(Bill Grundy was fired by Thames Television shortly after this incident, but a few years before his death, he returned to television, hosting a show where he visited various English country scenic sites and looked for the nearest pub.)

STeVe JONeS THERE WAS THIS RECEPTION AREA, AND ALL THE PHONES AND ALL THE LINES WERE JUST GOING... YOU KNOW, PEOPLE CALLING UP IN OUTRAGE. OH, IT WAS LIKE...OH, IT WAS EXCITING. I was fucking drunk—I was [makes drunklike noise], and it was great. And I had no idea what was going to happen the next day, you know. Had no idea. We were just in this little room with a camera and some guy who was being a cunt with us, and we coated him off.

JOHn LyDON IT ALIENATED THE ENTIRE COUNTRY, THE GRUNDY THING. The entire country, lock, stock and fucking barrel. Nothing left. If they had hung us at Traitor's Gate it would have been applauded by fifty-six million.

PaUL COOK I THINK I DIDN'T REALIZE THE SERIOUSNESS OF IT ALL. I didn't even know it was going out live, to tell you the truth—I don't think any of us did—but I think Malcolm realized it seriously, so we rushed out the studio back into the car and we didn't realize until the next day...We were totally oblivious to publicity that night...but the next morning there were reporters banging on the doors.

JOHn LyDON RIDICULOUS, TO HEAR OF PEOPLE KICKING IN THEIR TV SETS. Haven't they ever heard of the off button?

PaUL COOK

YEAH, MALCOLM WAS TOTALLY SHOCKED AT IT. But I think he did enjoy it the next day, once he realized the effect…Yeah, everything changed after the Grundy interview. Totally. It just totally changed our lives, really, I think—it really did. We were national news, international news, you know.

STeVe JONes

LIKE, SO OFTEN WE GOT SOME PRESS AND MORE PEOPLE STARTED TO TURN OUT THAT ACTUALLY STARTED TO LIKE US. We was that type of surprise because we were still learning to play. I don't think we were very good at the time ourselves.

JOHn LyDON

AFTER THE GRUNDY SHOW, NOTHING HAP-PENED FOR A LONG TIME. And you have to say, "Where's your management, mate?" Everything was, destructed. More money was spent on Malcolm having a very nice office than anything like, "Where's the rehearsal hall for the band?" It was a sleazeball office, but it was the best Malcolm deserved. It was vile…There was a limo after the Grundy show, but I was again dropped off somewhere, 'cause no one would take me home. But the next morning it was all over the newspapers. "Vile," "filthy," et cetera. The filthy lucre was just, coming into its own. Completely, from there on in, walking the streets of London on my own was impossible. I would be attacked on sight. It was that bad. It was extremely dangerous to do anything at all.

Cancelled t⊙ur dates.

PaUL COOK

WE WERE PUBLIC ENEMY NUMBER ONE, BUT ALSO NATIONAL HEROES TO A LOT OF PEOPLE AS WELL, YOU KNOW, TO A LOT OF KIDS. They loved it. They loved what we were doing especially— it split, really split really down the middle. It was one group of people that totally hated us and wanted to kill us, and then there was another group who were totally behind us and everything we were doing, the music, the image, the whole thing, the subculture, you know—everything.

STeVe JOnes

AND THEN IT WAS THAT WHOLE THING THEN IT WAS LIKE, BEING BANNED IN THIS TOWN AND BEING BANNED IN THAT TOWN. And it really wasn't about us playing anymore, it was about this, er, controversy, like we were throwing up onstage and spitting and...the *Sun*, the *Daily Mirror*, and all of them papers, just took it a lot further for selling papers' sake—for shock value...they, you know, they started inventing things they thought people wanted to read. To sell papers. I mean, we really wasn't as outrageous as they were saying at all.

JOHn LyDON

MOST INFAMOUS MAN IN THE COUNTRY, MR. ROTTEN—WITH NO MONEY. I still had to bunk on the subway, à la not pay—couldn't afford a cab, had no concept of rent. Squatting. It was fucked up— and very, very fucking dangerous and very violent.

PaUL COOK

YEAH, WE WERE OFF AFTER THE GRUNDY SHOW, WE HAD TO DO A TOUR, MOST OF WHICH WAS CANCELED, ALL THE PRESS WAS FOLLOWING US AROUND AND EVERYWHERE, WAITING FOR ANOTHER INCIDENT. We were selling loads of papers for them. This new phenomenon called Punk, that's what they called it.

ROCK CULT FILTH

CHEERS: Sex Pistols leader Johnny Rotten downs a beer after the show

When the air turned blue..

A POP group shocked millions of viewers last night with the filthiest language heard on British television.

By STUART GREIG.

Newspapers featuring the SEX PISTOLS on the front page regularly OUTSOLD the editions announcing the end of the SECOND WORLD WAR in 1945.

SLASHED

Razor attack on Rotten, the Punk Rocker

JOHNNY ROTTEN, king of

THE RECORD INDUSTRY NEVER GAVE US ANY HELP AT ALL, IN ANY SHAPE OR FORM. We'd always be a constant problem. I don't care whether that's Virgin or anybody. All of them. Once they'd signed us, they didn't know what to do with us. They didn't understand that free thought is where the industry's future lies. And to this day they've gone back to the old way, that's why everything now is so fucking dull, fake and shoddy. I got knifed and I got slashed and razored and all kind of things. But that's cool. I had to live with it. Because I knew I had no one to turn to.

EMI canceled
the SEX PISTOLS'
contract on
January 29,
1977, less than
two months
after the Grundy
interview.
The SEX PISTOLS
were allowed
to keep the
money paid them
by the record
company.

PaUL COOK

WELL, WE SIGNED TO A&M AFTER EMI KICKED US OFF—THEY DECIDED TO TAKE US ON AND... MALCOLM ORGANIZED THIS BIG THING, ACTUALLY SIGNING THE CONTRACT OUTSIDE OF BUCKINGHAM PALACE. It was all getting a bit wild, I suppose, really, by that time. And we did a press conference early in the morning at the hotel, this was really early—about ten o'clock, or even earlier, nine. All of the press were there to announce our signing...We all had a bit to drink, you know—I think Sid had been out for the night or whatever, he's a bit worse from it—and we're all in a terrible mood. The press conference was awful, we were just abusing everyone, you know, slagging everyone off, and that. Deteriorated into chaos. Then we got in the car and drove around to Buckingham Palace where we stumbled out of a car, make a quick signing of the contracts, got back in the car, and we was on our way again to the office of A&M to meet everybody. And on the way there we had a big argument in the car. It was quite serious, really.

JOHn LyDON

I DON'T REMEMBER WHAT IT WAS ABOUT. IT WAS ON THE LEVEL OF "YOU'RE A CUNT," "NO, YOU'RE A CUNT."

PaUL COOK

WHEN WE GOT TO A&M RECORDS, JUST A TOTAL BATTLE BROKE OUT. The secretaries were terrified and Sid was bleeding, his foot was bleeding like hell, Malcolm was running around, John was...Steve was swearing at all the secretaries. And then we got in the car again and went to the studio where we were recording "God Save the Queen," and there's a school next door to the studio and all the kids come running out of the school because we were there, and fights broke out and someone called the police because this was a primary school, and it was a total mad day.

A&M Records cancelled the SEX PISTOLS' contract later that year. Once again, the BAND was allowed to keep the substantial advance it had received.

PaUL COOK   **I THINK THE BEST TIME OF THE BAND WAS WHEN SID FIRST JOINED.** When he first joined the band, when he was really determined to learn the bass and to be part…I think that was the best time of the band. Livewise, it was really exciting, and he could play all right. We'd be touring, he'd learned the bass pretty quick—it was pretty simple stuff he was playing but it worked. John had pushed for Sid to be in the band. And he looked great and it was great. Really good. But it didn't last all that long because Sid started to go off the rails right away.

STeVe JONeS   **I DON'T KNOW IF HE [GLEN MATLOCK] CHANGED, OR IF IT WAS ME AND COOKIE AND JOHN WHO CHANGED.** It may have been the Grundy thing that had a lot to do with that. I don't know. I kind of regretted him [Glen] leaving after he left because, you know, Sid couldn't play a fucking

An animal? Not an animal? SiD ViCiOus.

I'M NOT AN ANIMAL

note and Sid was dark, man. He was a dark character and it wasn't fun anymore. The fun kind of left.
And he was Rotten's best friend and they were
always taking the piss...I always got the impression
they were taking the piss out of me. You know,
because I wasn't the brightest spark and they were
like arty guys and better than me.

The Sex Pistols signed with Richard Branson's
Virgin Records for good in May 1977.

SiD ViciOus **I'VE GOT THE MONIKER "VICIOUS"—I GOT THE
NAME VICIOUS BECAUSE I'M GANGLY AND
THIN AND MY FUCKING GIRLFRIEND CAN BEAT
ME AT ARM WRESTLING.**

JOHn LyDON

SID VICIOUS GOT THE NAME AFTER MY PET HAMSTER. I had a little white hamster that bit him one day when he was trying to be sweet to it—and his name was Sid and he really liked that. It was vicious, that. "Your Sid is vicious."

SiD ViciOus

BECAUSE OF MY NAME THEY ALL THINK, YOU KNOW, LIKE, IF THEY BEAT SID VICIOUS UP, THAT THEY'RE GONNA, YOU KNOW, PEOPLE ARE GONNA ADMIRE THEM, YOU KNOW, AND THINK THEY'RE WONDERFUL. Well, I'm not, I'm not a good fighter or anything like that, I'm not a good fighter but I *am* vicious—"vicious" is a good word to describe me—I'm not good at fighting but if I get somebody on the ground, then they are finished, d'you know what I mean? If, like, if I'm gonna... if I beat somebody—I beat them fucking bad.

JOHn LyDON

I'LL TELL YOU, TO THIS DAY I FEEL GUILTY ABOUT SID. I wish I had told him more about what to expect...He just had a brilliant sense of humor about everything. He'd just laugh at everything. Genius in that way. And be accurate in his humor. He would have a knack of just saying the right thing at the right time and it would be the truth. And it would be hilarious, too.

SiD ViciOus

ME AND JOHN ROTTEN, WE WERE ABOUT THE TWO FIRST REAL PUNKS IN LONDON. Greasy, dirty, nasty little bastards. Him with his yellow hair and me—I used to have it slicked back then, and we used to wear T-shirts with the sleeves rolled up, and fucking straight Levi's and baseball boots. Has anyone got a safety pin? Only to prick this blister.

What made the Sex Pistols different was John Rotten, really, because he was a total anti-star. He was a star, all right, but he was so...He didn't, like, wiggle his bum or shake his hips. He just did robot dancing and fucked around and took the piss out of everybody. In a real nasty, snidely way, he was fucking great. He was brilliant. The best...

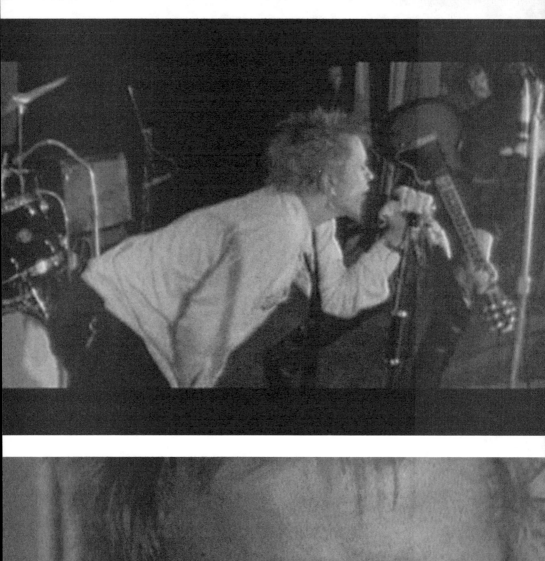

SiD ViciOus

WELL, I GOT NO RESPECT FOR HIM [JOHN LYDON] ANYMORE 'CAUSE HE FUCKED UP AND, LIKE, HE NEEDN'T HAVE FUCKED UP. He fucked the group up. They'll probably say that I did because of my drug habit and all that. But I played fucking sick, I spent a thirty-eight-hour coach [bus] ride sitting up, sick as a fucking dog. Sick like you wouldn't believe, unless you've been a junkie yourself. And, like, while they were all fucking sleeping, you know, and, like, I fucking went through pain like you wouldn't believe for that band—and, like, they were chasing me around every time I tried to get a fix, they'd like, be following me around and I'd just say, like, "Look, fuck off or otherwise someone's gonna get hurt," and then they'd leave me alone and I'd go and get my fix and that would be the end of it...

JOHn LyDOn

STEVE AND PAUL WERE ALWAYS INTO BEING ROCK STARS AND GETTING GROUPIES BACK-STAGE, AND STILL ARE. Steve and Paul just wanted groupies and fame. Glen wanted nice songs. Getting Sid in was to kind of change that situation somewhat. But Sid went straight into being the worst kind of rock-and-roll idiot you could ever hope to, like, have a nightmare about. It backfired on me. But it was still tolerable.

The band at Winterland.

SiD ViciOus

STEVE AND PAUL ARE A PAIR OF SHEEP. They do what Malcolm says, they just go along with anything he says. They're terrified of anything to do with drugs or, you know, blah, blah, anything like that. They're just wimps, you know what I mean?

Sex Pistols

The SPOTS
[SEX PISTOLS
On Tour in
Secret] Tour
began in
September of
1977.

STeve JOnes

I THINK THE BEST TOUR...THE BEST FUCKING TOUR WAS SPOTS [SEX PISTOLS ON TOUR IN SECRET]... AND WE JUST DID THESE SECRET GIGS AROUND THE NORTH OF ENGLAND AND I THINK A COUPLE OF SHOWS IN LONDON. But, kind of, kids knew. "Is it them? Is it them?" "Are they going to be playing?" And we played in the small clubs and it was just packed with, like, fans, who had never seen us up north and they were the best shows, man, they were fucking great...It was the best time for me. It was great. It was fucking great...

On Christmas
Day, 1977, the
SEX PISTOLS
played in the
northern
industrial
town of
Huddersfield,
Yorkshire.

Long-haired rocker John.

JOHn LyDOn

HUDDERSFIELD, I REMEMBER VERY FONDLY.
Two concerts, a matinee and a late-night one...It
was heaven personified. We were playing to hard-
core long-term prisoners—in that it was young kids
in the afternoon. All the orphanages, et cetera, et
cetera, and throwing pies at me, and later that night
the fire-engine people who had gone on strike and
they had organized all this—they were coming and
throwing custard tarts at us. Just genius. Just fun.
We were so hated at the time, but we were in touch
with young kids, easy. 'Cause we're honest. Nobody
gave a shit about all those working-class people
in that town—and we were there. We spent our
Christmas with orphans and striking union members,
children and adults in the evening and a lot of love
in the house...And Sid was great that night. That
day. Everything about it was just wonderful... And
that was the end of the band.

PaUL COOK

**WE PLAYED HUDDERSFIELD, CHRISTMAS DAY,
1977.** We'd been doing a few dates up until then.
I mean, around this time we wanted to be playing,
really, 'cause we were just getting into trouble hanging around doing nothing, you know, not cool. And
so we just wanted to be out of the way and playing,
really, so we were doing dates whenever we could,
which was quite hard anyway. But we managed to
get some dates leading up to Christmas Day, which
ended in Huddersfield, which ended up being a
benefit for the kids of firemen who were on strike
around that time, who'd been on strike for a long
time, and it was just a support for them, really, and
it turned out to be a really great gig. We'd done two
shows—one in the afternoon for the kids, a total
kids' thing, young kids—tykes there and everything.
We had flags and banners with pistols and all these
young kids waving *Never Mind the Bollocks* banners. We had the whole day of it. It was like our
Christmas party, really. I really remember everyone
being relaxed that day. Everyone was getting along
really well, everyone was in such a great mood.
Maybe it was just the Christmas spirit.

The Christmas
Day concert in
Huddersfield
would be the
last played
by the SEX
PISTOLS in
the U.K.

PaUL COOK

I HAD NO IDEA IT WAS OUR LAST GIG IN ENGLAND. Things had been pretty tense up until then, but everyone was really relaxed on that tour. I think we was just glad to be out of the way then, playing again. Playing in the band on the road, you know. Being together, really. And Sid was there, he was with Nancy, you know, he was happy enough, and we was all having a good time, really, and we felt good doing the gig for the firemen and stuff. I think it was one of our, you know, rememberable gigs. Really was.

The
SEX PISTOLS'
American
concert tour
began in
ATLANTA,
Georgia, on
January 3,
1978.

STEVE JONES

WE DIDN'T UNDERSTAND AMERICA. SO HOW THE FUCK COULD THEY UNDERSTAND US?

PAUL COOK

THEN, A WEEK LATER [AFTER HUDDERSFIELD], WE GOT THE STATES TOUR ORGANIZED AGAIN, BUT WE DIDN'T REALLY REALIZE WHAT THAT WAS GOING TO BE LIKE. Just after getting over all the "God Save the Queen" stuff...It was all dying down a little bit after Christmas and everything was kind of getting all right again. We were right back in it again in America—even more so, you know. Right back, full-on in-your-face publicity people following us about, and everyone getting paranoid and tense again. Straight back into it again, you know, when we could have done without it, really, I think. And we had trouble getting visas because we all had criminal records—all of us—and we were refused working visas, which was another scandal in the press, you know, we had to cancel a few of the dates, 'cause we arrived late in the States. So we ended up starting the tour in Georgia, of all places—Atlanta. And we had the press and everything following us around there because all the publicity preceded us, obviously, and it was back to square one again, if you like.

JOHN LYDON

THEY STRIP-SEARCHED US AT THE AIRPORT AND, THANK GOD, SID WAS THE FIRST ONE THEY STRIP-SEARCHED, BECAUSE AS SOON AS THEY SEEN HIS UNDERWEAR, THAT WAS IT, WE WERE SAFE. They had no wish to play with the rest of our willies after that point.

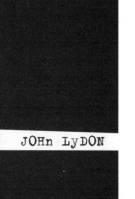

STEVE AND PAUL FLEW AROUND AMERICA WITH MALCOLM BECAUSE THEY DIDN'T WANT TO BE ON THE TOUR BUS. To me it was the best tour I'd ever had. It was my first time in America and Sid would sit next to me and we'd look out the window and we'd stare at endless scenery and imagine John Wayne and the Indians.

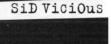

OH, AMERICAN AUDIENCES ARE JUST THE SAME AS ANYBODY ELSE. Except a bit more boring. They're not as boring as Swedish audiences, though.

BECAUSE OF THE DRUGS, WE TRAVELED ON THE BUS. I thought it would work. This is why Sid was to stick with me. But it didn't happen that way.

THE BAND BROKE UP BECAUSE I COULDN'T BEAR ROTTEN ANYMORE, BECAUSE HE WAS AN EMBARRASSMENT WITH HIS SILLY HATS AND HIS, LIKE, SHABBY, NASTY, DIRTY-LOOKING APPEARANCE. He just didn't.... At one time that guy looked like a shining star, you know what I mean? Like he shone. When he walked down the street you could see him coming, he had an aura around him, he was somebody. Mister John Rotten. You know what I mean? *Mister* John Rotten. But, like, now he's just, like, you know, he could be fuck-ing Joe Bloggs in the street. That's how mundane he is now. I still like him but I've got no respect for him. I wish I could, I wish I could still be friends with him. I'm really upset about it.

LONGHORN
Ballroom

TONITE
SEX PISTOLS
MERLE HAGGARD

JOHn LyDON

AND IN MY WILDEST, WORST NIGHTMARE FAN-TASIES, I WOULD NEVER HAVE THOUGHT THAT ENGLISH PEOPLE COULD EVER HAVE DISRE-SPECTED THEMSELVES TO THE POINT WHERE HEROIN WAS THEIR BE-ALL AND END-ALL. What a loser, self-pitying bunch of fucking shit. I hate, loathe, and despise them. I despise Sid for it.

STeVe JONeS

WELL, COMING TO AMERICA WAS DEFINITELY, ER, A STRANGE EXPERIENCE. Continually followed by the FBI and the fucking CIA and fifty journalists and all these other people trying to leech off our fame. And it was just paranoia. Here, like, we had these bodyguards, the walkie-talkies and that, and it was kind of scary in a way, and I don't know what it was, man, but it fucking drew us all apart. Rotten got into his ego, Sid was just looking for smack—being an idiot—and it got real depressing real quick in America.

SiD ViciOus

I WASN'T REAL IMPRESSED WITH AMERICA UNTIL I GOT TO FRISCO AND WE MET SOME KIDS AND TASTED THE SMACK THERE. Fucking straight from Mexico—real pure. It's really fucking good. You should try it sometime.

STeVe JONeS

I DIDN'T GET THE IMPRESSION THAT SOMEONE WAS GOING TO KILL US...I'M SURE THERE WERE SOME IDIOTS OUT THERE WHO WERE THINKING ABOUT IT. 'Cause America is the land of fucking loonies with guns who kill people...But the birds were better-looking here, though, in America, that's for sure. Groovy, groovy chicks. Much better than the fat slags from up north in England. You know, I liked that, I really enjoyed that part of it. They know how to suck dick in America. They learn at an early age here, you know.

JOHn LyDON

AND THEN WE GOT TO SAN FRANCISCO...AND SUDDENLY SID COMES BACK SMACKED UP . . . And that was the end of Sid and that was the last gig and that was it. And that's why I said, "Ever get the feeling you've been cheated?"

STeVe JONes

I WAS JUST NOT HAPPY. I was just getting more and more where I wanted out of the band until we got to San Francisco, and that's when I said, "I don't want to do it no more."

JOHn LyDON

HE [SID] TURNED TO ARROGANCE AND SELF-IMPORTANCE WHEN HE WAS INFLUENCED BY DRUGS. Arrogance and self-importance are delicious tools that I use very well, but Sid couldn't quite match that. He was trying to be Johnny Rotten.

STeVe JONes

WELL, SID WASN'T EVEN PLAYING AT THE END. He could barely play anyway, and he just started thinking he was DeeDee Ramone, you know. And he couldn't even fucking...wasn't even playing—half the time he wasn't even plugged in, you know? It was like a joke, it was like, "What the fuck am I up here for? What am I doing?" With this just this kind of fucking kind of circus—you know—it became like a circus and I just didn't want any part of it, really... I really don't think it would have lasted, you know, even though I regret not trying to make it...See, I thought we could take it...[But] I really don't think it was going anywhere.

I REGRET SAYING THAT, THAT I WANTED OUT AND WAS LEAVING. I regret...I really do. I apologize to John and...that I fucking bailed on him because we might have continued if we had got rid of Malcolm. But that's just the way I felt—that I couldn't get away from my feeling at the time.

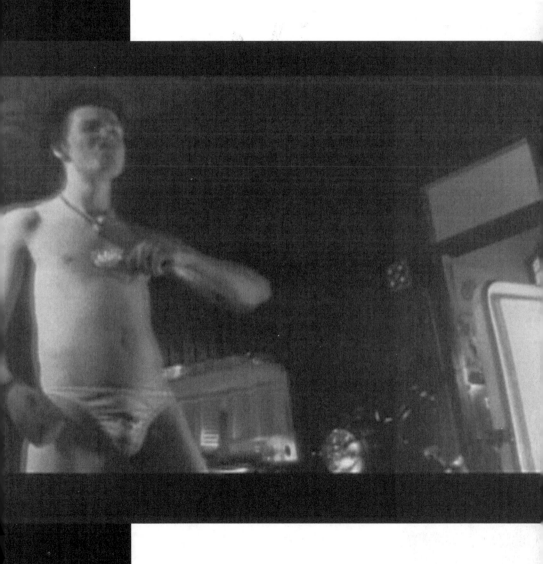

The
SEX PISTOLS
played their
last concert
in SAN
FRANCISCO on
January 14,
1978.

NOWHER

The Pistols' "Nowhere"
bus moved some of them
acrOss the States.

SiD ViCiOus — WELL, YOU KNOW, LIKE, I DON'T GIVE A FUCK WHAT THE GENERAL PUBLIC THINK. They're just like scum to me—they don't mean shit to me. They're just dirt off the street. You know, I live my life my way, you know, and that's all there is to it. They can do what they want, I'll do what I want.

STeVe JONes — IT'S BEEN SINCE THE BEGINNING OF TIME— EVERYONE KNOWS WHEN A BIRD STARTS POK- ING HER NOSE INTO A ROCK-AND-ROLL BAND, IT'S FUCKING SUICIDAL, YOU KNOW. It always has been, and because we were Punk and a new thing, it was no different in that aspect of it, you know. And I gather she [Nancy Spungen] introduced him [Sid] to heroin, because that's when he started to get fucked up and not caring about playing.

JOHn LyDON — I THINK SID HAD A FEAR INSIDE HIMSELF. He had a lack of self-esteem, and maybe in weird ways it was wrong chucking him into the Sex Pistols because he couldn't cope with it from that side of the fence. Sid loved the Pistols as a fan—being onstage with us, he couldn't cope. He couldn't get round the fact that he...then...that he had to be on an equal footing with us and, er, would justify himself through competing—because he couldn't compete.

SiD ViCiOus — ONCE YOU'VE PUT A NEEDLE IN YOUR ARM, YOU'RE HEADING FOR SMACK. That's where you end up. You know...I can handle it. I'm on methadone now, I'm curing myself. And then, after that, I'll just get off occasionally. I won't get myself a habit. And then I'll be able to work okay...I don't want to be a junkie for the rest of my life. I don't want to be a junkie at all. I mean, I'm not ashamed of it but I don't want to be a junkie. I don't want to be tied down to something.

Sex Pistols

PaUL COOK

THE FIRST TIME I CAME ACROSS NANCY, I THINK STEVE WAS SHAGGING HER IN THE TOILET.
That's when I first saw her...I didn't like her. She's an American, you know, and how Sid got involved with her, I'll never know. John got Sid involved in the band so that he could have someone to hang around with. Nancy comes along and she's the one Sid's off with, doing drugs.

Nancy Spungen.

Sid in front of McLaren's Sex Shoppe.

Nancy
Spungen

I READ THE FIRST SEX PISTOLS' REVIEW, WHICH WAS SHIT, AND I SAID, "I GOT TO GET OVER THERE." So I saved all my money fourteen times, fourteen times I spent on smack...I had it all saved up like, five thousand dollars, and *bam!* it went in a week. Like, you know, I was fucking horrible—so I worked straight for eleven days and got the money to come over and I came finally after that...I stayed with a good friend of mine called Linda, and Sid just happened to be staying there at the same time— and you could say that we've been living together since the day I got here, really.

JOHn LyDON

YOU MUST UNDERSTAND, NANCY, AS HIS HEROIN-STROKE-GIRLFRIEND, WAS PUMPING HIM UP WITH GEAR EVERY CHANCE SHE COULD GET. The idea was to keep her away from that. What she was constantly telling Sid was that he was the true star and I was a cunt and an arsehole. She might be right. But the point is, Sid's my mate and I don't want him to be a junkie. He was far too young for that shit…That's…un-American for that shit if you know what I'm talking about—and I wouldn't be tolerating that. I look out for my mates. Call me a problem for that, but there it is.

Nancy sPunGeN

I WAS SO FUCKING SICK WHEN I FIRST GOT THERE. I WAS SO SICK. I was just really sick. I was really sick until I got a connection. It took me about six or seven months to make a good connection, even. In New York you go down to the Bowery and just walk into a social club or a delicatessen and you just tell them how much you want and you hand them the money and they hand you the dope and you walk out. And it's like, two seconds. But over here you gotta…you know…it's like a whole mishmash.

PaUL COOK

COMING TO NEW YORK AND SEEING A LOT— THAT'S WHEN HEAVY DRUGS WERE GOING BOLD, THAT INFLUENCED A LOT OF THINGS, ESPECIALLY WITH SID, WATCHING HIM GOING OUT DOWN WITH NANCY AND THE HEROIN. It was just a running battle all the time, really.

Nancy sPunGeN

I'VE ALWAYS BEEN AROUND MUSIC, I KNOW THE BUSINESS INSIDE OUT. I wanted to manage a band. I've been telling Sid from the minute he was in the Pistols, "Don't do that because you're going to get yourself in that position. Get this check with this solicitor [lawyer] because you're going to get caught in this way." I know it. I know the business. So I'd like to put it to some use.

SiD ViciOus

ROTTEN TURNED AGAINST ME AND HE THOUGHT THAT I WAS TRYING TO TAKE OVER FROM HIM, BECAUSE I LEAPED ABOUT ONSTAGE AND GIRLS LIKE ME AND STUFF...HE THOUGHT I WAS TRY-ING TO TAKE OVER HIS POSITION AS THE "NEW JOHNNY ROTTEN," WAS THE WAY HE PUT IT...AND LIKE, THAT'S A LOAD OF COBBLERS. I was just playing bass and fucking going crazy leaping up and down, you know what I mean.

GLeN MaTLOCk

SID BECAME A MORE OF A CELEBRITY THAN JOHN. And that's why it broke up. You don't need more than one lead singer in a band. Or one strong character in a band. I was always quite happy to be one of the Indians.

NaNCy SPuNGeN

AS FAR AS SID GOES, HE WAS A HOT, HOT NUMBER WITH THE GIRLS OVER THERE. And they all wanted to know what was John's phone number and where he lived.

STeVe JONes

FIRST TIME I REMEMBER MEETING HER [Spungen] WAS...ER...WE PLAYED AT THE NOTRE DAME HALL UP THE WEST END AND SHE SHOWED UP WITH SID AT A SOUND CHECK AND I WAS THINKING, "WHO THE FUCK IS THIS CUNT? THIS IS A HORRIBLE PERSON." It was just a dark cloud with this bird. It was the weirdest thing. I never felt an energy—a negative energy—from someone, from this bird, and she would want to be everywhere with Sid. I fucking hated her.

Sex Pistols

Nancy
Spungen

I HAVEN'T FUCKED ALL THE SEX PISTOLS. Just Sid and Steve, and the only reason I did Steve was because I went to see Sid in hospital when he was sick and he said, "I bet you any amount of money the next time you see Steve he's gonna put the make on you." And I went to the Clash party after they played at the Rainbow, and sure enough, the first thing, Steve comes all the way across the room to me. "Let's go outside, Nancy. Or let's go in the bathroom." I said, "No, take me back to your house, I'm not an in-the-bathroom fucker anymore, you know."

JOHn LyDOn

WHATEVER HAPPENED TO BABY JANE WAS NANCY. That was the vicious old cow...Bette Davis. Yes, Nancy was Bette Davis. And isn't it peculiar that all these years later that you get someone looking up to Nancy as a hero? Are we talking about that whore bitch?

NaNcy sPunGen

SID'S GOT HIS OWN KINKS. I mean, I'm not going to put my private life on film. I mean, what we do in bed is private to me and Sid. But I mean, fucking Steve was...like..."suck my cock again" and "let's fuck again"—all night long. Aaaarrrhhh, leave me alone!

JOHn LyDON

SID'S MOTHER WAS FURIOUS WITH NANCY BECAUSE SHE WAS TRASH AND JUST *BANG, BANG, BANG.* I can't explain heroin culture to you...But two women and a gram of smack and a young boy, one being the son, one being the girl-friend, is a very, very volatile situation. They're not arguing over the kitchen sink anymore. You can imagine what hell went on in there. And Sid's endless screaming, "Get me out of here."

NanCy SPunGen

IF I MANAGED THE SEX PISTOLS, I'D SAVE THEIR FUCKING PRIVATE LIVES. Give them a bank account. Maybe put it all in a trust or something. Give them a bank account and a checkbook and let them...If they spend all their money that's their fault. You know what I mean? That's the way every-body else is run. Why...you know, Malcolm is just being...he's a cunt. He's good with media, you know, but he really didn't do anything with the media. They did it all for him. Really. The whole thing with the papers and stuff. He's good like that. He's good getting contracts but other than that, he's...I don't see him good at anything at all, as far as managing goes. He just comes up with complete-ly ludicrous ideas, that absolutely won't come off, that are absolutely stupid and disgusting.

SHE WAS THE ULTIMATE JUNKIE BITCH, LOSER, SPITEFUL COW FROM HELL. And [she] bragged about it. Do me a fucking favor. Talk about getting it wrong. Cor, what a fucking toilet.

Nancy Spungen was found STABBED to death in the Chelsea Hotel, New York City, on November 11, 1978. SID VICIOUS was charged with her murder.

SID
VICIOUS
died of
a drug
overdose on
February 2,
1979:

I didn't
Nancy, s
Sid Vicio

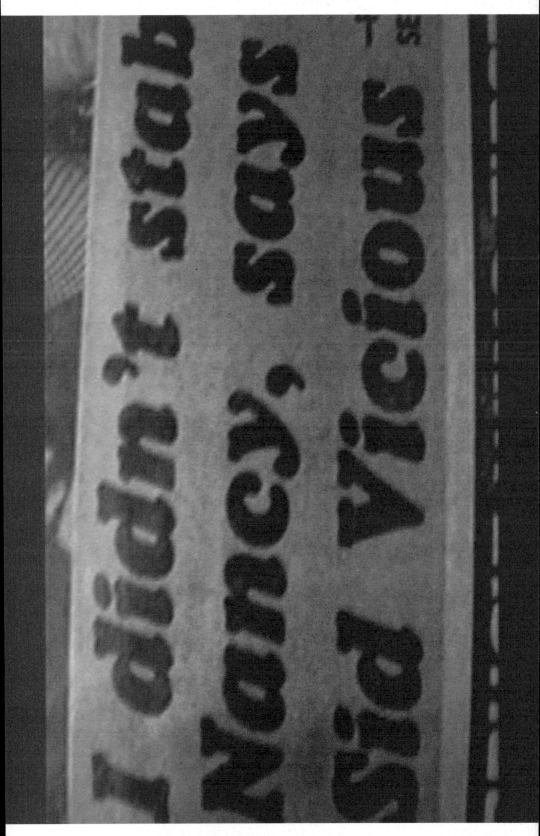

JOHn LyDON

I FEEL NOTHING BUT GRIEF, SORROW, AND SADNESS FOR SID. To the point that, if I really, talk about it, I just fucking burst into tears. He's someone I really cared for, see. I don't care that much about any of the Sex Pistols that way…I couldn't have changed it. I was too young. God, I wish I was smarter, you know. You can look back on it and go, "I could have done something"…He died, for fuck's sake. And they just turned it into making money, ha ha ha. How hilarious for them. Fucking cheat! I'll hate them forever for doing that. You can't get more evil than that, can you, really? You know, no respect…Vicious. Poor sod.

STeve JONes

I DIDN'T GIVE A FUCK AT THE TIME OF SID'S DEATH. I just thought, "Oh well, we'll probably sell more records now"…What would Sid have done if he wasn't in a band? What would he have become? He was definitely a drug addict. He'd probably be dead anyway.

JOHn LyDON

IS THERE A BOND WITH THE SEX PISTOLS? I don't know. To this day…to this day, I love and hate them at the same time. And I'm sure that's their feelings about me. I don't know if they could be as honest as me about it. I knew what Steve was and I liked him and I knew he had the potential to be a great person. He always will be, in his way. A great person. There's something in him that's genuine. He just gets confused.

Sid had been arraigned and was
out on bail when he died.

IN ENGLAND IT'S COLD AND MISERABLE. No one had any jobs. You couldn't get any jobs. Everyone was on the dole. There was no future...you know, if you weren't born into money then you might as well kiss your fucking life good-bye...And in America it was a lot different. You could be a complete fucking nobody and make a million dollars. It was a lot more easier to do that in America. You couldn't do that in England. With John, I have mixed feelings. One part of me really loves him, but...and then, the other side of me can't stand him. You know, I think he's not growing old gracefully. I think he's still saying the same shtick and pulling

Cook, Lydon, and Matlock in an early rehearsal

the same shit that he used to pull twenty years ago and it don't work now and he's fucking...you know, he's forty...you know, forty-odd now and, er, it annoys me to see him like that. It fucking hurts me to see him just make a fucking cunt of himself. I think alcohol's got a lot to do with it. I think he's got the same problem as me but he's not willing to accept that, and he's in denial about it. And we had our moment and it was a great fucking moment, you know. Anything else after that is icing on the cake. You know.

PaUL COOK **I THINK THE SEX PISTOLS ARE MORE RELEVANT NOW THAN THEY WERE WHEN THEY WERE TOGETHER, REALLY.** Any band that's came along in the last fucking fifteen years has definitely been inspired by the Sex Pistols and they come up and tell me, "Oh, you've changed my life, blah, blah, blah, blah." It took a new dimension onto music when we came along...It opened up a whole new world to music to where you could go, and attitude, and...just anything can go...The Sex Pistols has been one of the most important bands in music— as far as I'm concerned. And that was just meant to be, that one album...

STeVe JONeS

I REALLY BELIEVE WE WERE MEANT TO DO THAT ONE RECORD AND BREAK UP. I believe that's what the plan was. You know. Yeah. We gave it fucking two hundred percent for two years and that was it. It had run out of steam quick. I loved being a Sex Pistol, I'll always be a Sex Pistol.

GLeN MaTLOCk

IT'S A BIG ALBATROSS, YOU KNOW. Everybody wants to be part of a band, wants to know you for being part of a band, and they won't let you get on with your own stuff. It's very hard to escape from being a Sex Pistol. But that's the way it is. You know, I wouldn't have missed it for the world and I wouldn't have not backed out when I did. I mean, you can't change the way things go and I'm quite laissez-faire about things as far as that's concerned. And it's all part of "life's rich pageant" if you want to call it. But yeah, it does grind you down sometimes.

Paul Cook live.

Sex Pistols

I FELT CHEATED. I FELT RIPPED OFF AND CHEATED. And that's how I feel about the Sex Pistols. Ripped off and cheated. Lied to, faked to. Too much industry was allowed into it. Too much middle-class bullshit, bollocks. I've never been given any fucking respect here. And why the fucking hell should I care?

STeVe JONeS

WE DIDN'T UNI[...]
SO HOW THE FU[...]
UNDERSTAND U[...]

RSTAND AMERICA.
K COULD THEY
?

NORWICH ... FRI DEC

CARDIFF ... SAT DEC

NEWCASTLE ... DEC

LEEDS ... BOXING DEC

BOURNEMOUTH ... DEC

MANCHESTER
Electric Circus ... THU 9 DEC

LIVERPOOL ... DEC

OUR
TS